THE 7 HABITS OF
Highly Effective Teens
ON THE GO

Wisdom for Teens to Build Confidence, Stay Positive, and Live an Effective Life

SEAN COVEY

THE 7 HABITS OF Highly Effective Teens ON THE GO

Welcome to *The 7 Habits of Highly Effective Teens on the Go*

In this compact book you are holding, I'm inviting you to become a more mindful and effective individual. Each section contains wisdom to help you to become a better version of you, improve your relationships (including the one you have with yourself), and ways to effect more positive change in your life.

You're probably thinking, *Yeah, right, Sean. I have so much going on right now I don't have time to take on ONE more thing.* But that's the very reason we created this book. It's on the go, quick, and effective. Just take a few minutes once a week to read a section, reflect on it, and accept the challenge presented to you. You can do this while you're waiting for your friends to pick you up, while you're waiting in line somewhere, or waiting for your computer or phone to update (again).

Introduction to the Habits

Now hear me out. If you promise to do the weekly challenges, I'll promise to make it fun. The information on each card is all taken from my internationally bestselling book, *The 7 Habits of Highly Effective Teens*. Maybe you read the book in school, maybe your parents required you to read it before you could learn to drive, or maybe you've never read the book at all—either way, the same message is presented in a fresh and easily manageable way. I break down each of the 7 Habits simply and offer methods to apply the lessons into your daily routine and thought patterns.

If you're the kind of person who prefers to skip around, that's just fine. Do it your way, but stick with it—you'll be glad you did. Never forget that out of small changes, big things are achieved.

If you do this, and work hard to move out of your comfort zone and shift your belief systems, then I promise that you'll improve and repair your relationships, and you'll become a more effective young adult. And effectiveness leads to success in life—I know, that's a big promise.

I wish you all the best on your journey,

SEAN COVEY

Introduction to the Habits

The 7 Habits can help you:

- Take control of your life
- Improve your relationships with your friends
- Make smarter decisions
- Get along with your parents
- Find balance between school, work, friends, and family
- Get more done in less time
- Achieve a balanced, happy frame of mind

Now let's get started!

Introduction to the Habits

The 7 Habits of Highly Effective Teens

Habit 1 Be Proactive

Take responsibility for your life. You are not a victim of genetics, circumstance, or upbringing. Live life from your Circle of Influence.

Habit 2 Begin With the End in Mind

Define your values, mission, and goals in life. Live life based upon your vision of your life.

Habit 3 Put First Things First

Prioritize your activities and focus on what matters most. Spend more of your time in Quadrant II: the quadrant of important but not urgent.

Habit 4 Think Win-Win

Have an everyone-can-win attitude; be happy for the success of others.

Habit 5 Seek First to Understand, Then to Be Understood

Listen to people empathically and then ask to be heard.

Habit 6 Synergize

Value and celebrate differences so that you can achieve more than you ever could have alone.

Habit 7 Sharpen the Saw

Consistently recharge your batteries in all four dimensions: physical, mental, spiritual, and social/emotional.

Week 1

Get in the Habit

Habits are things we do repeatedly. But most of the time we are hardly aware that we have them because we're on autopilot. Some habits are good, some are bad, and some don't really matter. Depending on what they are, our habits will either make us or break us. Luckily, you are stronger than your habits and you can change them.

Introduction to the Habits

Ask yourself:

What habits do I have? Are they good or bad? Or neutral?

Make a list of two good habits and two bad habits. Next to each good habit comment on how you can strengthen and grow that habit. Next to each bad habit, comment on what you can do to change the habit into a productive one.

Introduction to the Habits

Week 2

Build Habit Momentum

The habits build upon each other. Habits 1, 2, and 3 deal with self-mastery—this skill is called the Private Victory. Habits 4, 5, and 6 deal with relationships and teamwork. It's called the Public Victory. Habit 7 is the habit of renewal, it feeds all of the other six habits.

Introduction to the Habits

Ask yourself:

Do I spend more time concerned about others' behavior than I do my own? Do I tend to think the problem is "out there" rather than considering my own behavior?

Study the order of The 7 Habits. Draw your own conclusions as to why they are in the order they are in.

Week 3

Paradigms and Principles

Paradigms are like glasses. When you have incomplete paradigms about yourself or life in general, it's like wearing glasses with the wrong prescription. That lens affects how you see everything else. If you believe you're unintelligent, that very belief will make you so. If you believe you're intelligent, that belief will cast a rosy hue on everything you do.

Introduction to the Habits

Ask yourself:

Where in my life do I have the most problems—in my relationships? My self-worth? My attitude?

The next time you complain about something or someone you can't control, stop and ask yourself, "Why am I concerned about that? Is there anything I can do to change that paradigm?"

Introduction to the Habits

Week 4

The Paradigms of Others

We not only have paradigms about ourselves, but also about other people. Seeing things from a different point of view can help us understand why other people act the way they do. We too often judge people without having all the facts.

Introduction to the Habits

Ask yourself:

What information might I be missing from a challenge I'm facing with someone right now?

The next time you find yourself in a complicated or uncomfortable situation with another person, challenge yourself to put a new lens on it. Ask for more information before making a judgment.

Introduction to the Habits

Week 5

Becoming Principle-Centered

Just as there are principles that rule the physical world, there are principles that rule the human world. Principles are not religious. Principles don't have a nationality. They apply to everyone, regardless of social status or gender. Honesty is a principle. Service is a principle. Respect, gratitude, moderation, fairness, integrity, loyalty, and responsibility are principles.

Introduction to the Habits

Ask yourself:

What do I value most? What three principles are most important to me? Do I center my life around those principles?

When you do your homework, chores, and/or practice tonight, try out the principle of hard work. Go the extra mile and do more than is expected.

Introduction to the Habits

Week 6

Your Personal Bank Account

How you feel about yourself is like a bank account—a Personal Bank Account (PBA). Just like an account at a bank, you can make deposits into and take withdrawals from your PBA by the things you think, say, and do.

For example, when I stick to a commitment I've made to myself, it's a deposit. When I break a promise to myself, I feel disappointed and make a withdrawal.

Introduction to the Habits

Ask yourself:

How is my personal bank account (PBA)? How much trust and confidence do I have in myself?

Identify one easy task that needs to be done today. Decide when you will do it. Now, keep your word and get it done.

Introduction to the Habits

Week 7

Deposits and Withdrawals

PBA Deposits

Keep promises to yourself

Do small acts of kindness

Be gentle with yourself

Be honest

Renew yourself

PBA Withdrawals

Break personal promises

Be unkind or rude to others

Beat yourself up

Lie to yourself or others

Wear yourself out

Introduction to the Habits

Ask yourself:

How am I feeling about myself? Do I make more deposits than withdrawals?

Make a list of deposits you make to yourself. Now make a list of the withdrawals. Set a specific goal about how you can change the withdrawals to deposits.

Introduction to the Habits

Check Your Balance

Week 8

Personal Bank Account

Introduction to the Habits

Ask yourself:

What do I need to work on? Instead of just writing the areas you have trouble with, write the solutions. For example, instead of "I'm always late," write "Practice leaving fifteen minutes earlier every day."

_____
_____
_____
_____
_____
_____
_____
_____
_____

Introduction to the Habits

Week 9

Habit 1: Be Proactive

Be Proactive is the key to unlocking all the other habits and that's why it comes first. Habit 1 says, "I am the force. I am the captain of my own life. I can choose my attitude. I am responsible for my own happiness or unhappiness."

Ask yourself:

Am I easily offended? Do I take responsibility for my choices? Do I think before I act? Do I focus on things I can do something about?

Write yourself a sticky note that says: "I will not let _____ decide how I am going to feel."

Determine what events and people trigger you to react negatively. Now be prepared so at the next trigger event you can repeat to yourself what you wrote on the sticky note.

Habit 1: Be Proactive

Week 10

Proactive and Reactive Words

Reactive Language

I'll try

That's just the way I am

There's nothing I can do

I have to

You ruined my day

Proactive Language

I'll do it

I can do better than that

Let's look at all our options

I choose to

I'm not going to let your bad mood rub off on me

Habit 1: Be Proactive

Ask yourself:

How do I respond to others? Do I tend to be more proactive or reactive?

The next time someone flips you off, give them a peace sign!

Habit 1: Be Proactive

Week 11

Listen to Your Language

Reactive language takes power away from you and gives it to something or someone else. Reactive language sounds like this:

- "You make me so..."
- "There's nothing I can do"
- "That's just the way I am"
- "I can't"

Habit 1: Be Proactive

Ask yourself:

How many times have I been driving when suddenly somebody cuts in front of me? What do I do? Do I curse and scream at the driver? Flip them off? Or do I just let it go and move on?

Listen carefully to your words today. Count how many times you use reactive language, such as:

- "You make me so…"
- "I have to…"
- "I can't…"

When you hear yourself using reactive language, immediately replace it with proactive language.

Habit 1: Be Proactive

Week 12

Becoming a Change Agent

Bad habits such as abuse, alcoholism, and other addictions are often passed down from parents to kids, and dysfunctional families keep repeating themselves. The good news is that you can stop the cycle. You can become a "change agent" and pass on good habits to future generations.

Habit 1: Be Proactive

Ask yourself:

Am I a "victim" of my upbringing? What would I like to change about my family dynamics? How can I be a change agent in my family now?

Choose a person you admire. What qualities do they have that you'd like to have? Interview that person and ask how they became who they are today.

Habit 1: Be Proactive

Week 13

Circle of Concern

Circle of No Control

Reactions
Choices
CIRCLE of CONTROL
Attitudes
Ourselves

Color of Eyes · Weather · Past Mistakes
Cost of Tuition · Parents · Rude Comments
Location of Birth · Who Will Win NBA Finals

A "Circle of Concern," or "Circle of Control," contains the things you can influence. You have the power to make a difference in these areas! That is why you should focus on them the most, instead of wasting time on your Circle of No Control, which is made of things simply out of your reach. The graphic above shows examples of what each of these might be.

Habit 1: Be Proactive

Challenge yourself:

Fill in the circle below with the things in your life that are not in your control, and those that are.

Habit 1: Be Proactive

Week 14

Habit 2: Begin with the End in Mind

Habit 2: Begin With the End in Mind means developing a clear picture of where you want to go with your life. It means deciding what your values are and setting goals. If Habit 1 says you are the driver of your life, Habit 2 says decide where you want to go and draw a map to get there.

Ask yourself:

Have I given much thought to my future? To where I want to go and what I want to be? Am I aware of what it takes to get there?

Think about your life goals. Think of where you want to be in five years, ten years, and twenty years. Write down three goals for each.

Habit 2: Begin With the End in Mind

Week 15

The Crossroads of Life

The paths you choose today can shape you forever. It's both frightening and exciting that you have to make so many vital decisions while you're young and full of life.

Habit 2: Begin With the End in Mind

Ask yourself:

Which path do I want to take in regards to drugs, career, college, sex, attitude, values, friends, and family relationships?

Think about a crossroad in your life you are facing right now. Determine right now which path would be best to take, write it down, and post it where you can see it often.

Week 16

A Personal Mission Statement

A personal mission statement is the best way to determine your End in Mind. A personal mission statement is like a credo or motto that states what your life is about. It is the blueprint to your life.

Habit 2: Begin With the End in Mind

Ask yourself:

What am I good at? What is most important to me? What do I love to do? Who inspires me?

Go to a quiet and private place and think deeply about who you are and what makes you unique. Write a first draft of a personal mission statement. Revisit it after you've had time to sleep on it.

Habit 2: Begin With the End in Mind

Week 17

The Great Discovery

A personal mission statement is like a tree with deep roots. It's going to be continually growing, but it also helps you stay stable through all of the storms of life. Part of discovering these roots is knowing what your strengths and interests are.

Habit 2: Begin With the End in Mind

Ask yourself:

What do I absolutely love to do? What symbol or thing represents me? Is it a guitar, a garden, a candle, an animal? Why does it represent me?

Think about a time you were deeply inspired. Where were you? What were you doing?

Habit 2: Begin With the End in Mind

Week 18

What's Important to You?

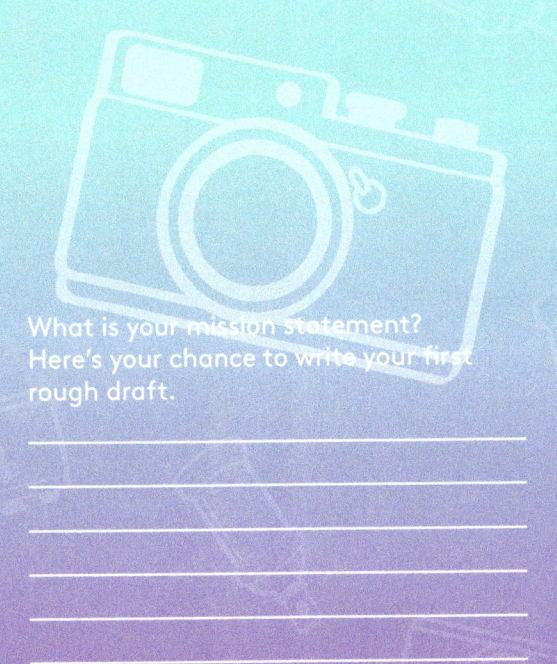

What is your mission statement? Here's your chance to write your first rough draft.

_____
_____
_____
_____
_____
_____

Habit 2: Begin With the End in Mind

Ask yourself:

What person has had a positive influence on my life? Who was it and what qualities do they possess that I would like to develop?

- Describe a time you were deeply inspired.
- List three things you love to do.
- If you could spend one hour with any person who ever lived, who would it be? What would you ask them?

Habit 2: Begin With the End in Mind

Week 19

Habit 3: First Things First

Habit 3: First Things First is all about learning to prioritize and manage your time so that your first things—your goals and plans—come first, not last. Putting first things first also deals with learning to overcome your fears and being strong during hard moments.

Habit 3: Put First Things First

Ask yourself:

Do I prioritize what's most important in my life? Do I plan my life or does my life just happen to go with the flow?

For a full day track where you spend your time. Do it in increments of thirty minutes. Be honest with yourself.

Habit 3: Put First Things First

Get Into Action

Week 20

My father, Stephen R. Covey, once said, "The main thing is to keep the main thing the main thing."

Habit 3: Put First Things First

Ask yourself:

What does this quote mean to me?

What "main things" do you want to focus on every day? Write it on this card. Put this card somewhere you will see it often.

Habit 3: Put First Things First

Week 21

The Comfort Zone and The Courage Zone

Your comfort zone represents things you're familiar with, activities you enjoy doing. It's easy. It doesn't require any stretching. In the Courage Zone is uncertainty, pressure, change, the fear of failure. But it's also the place of opportunity and growth.

Habit 3: Put First Things First

Ask yourself:

Do I let my fears make my decisions? Do I venture outside my comfort zone to make new friends, resist peer pressure, develop a new skill, or break an old habit?

Identify a fear that is holding you back from doing something you've always wanted to do. List all of the things you need to do to take that first step.

Habit 3: Put First Things First

Week 22

Taking Risks

Courage Zone

Things I Enjoy Doing
Relaxation · Ease
COMFORT
Freedom from Risk **ZONE** Safety & Security
Things I'm Accustomed To
Surety

Things I'm Afraid of · Things I've Never Tried · Risk
Hard Moments · Ultimate Potential · Unexplored Territory
Things That Are Difficult · Opportunity · Bravery · Higher Duty · Adventure

Putting first things first takes courage and will often cause you to stretch outside your comfort zone.

Habit 3: Put First Things First

Ask yourself:

When did I last do something out of my comfort zone? Did it hurt? Why don't I do it more often?

Courage Zone

COMFORT ZONE

You might ask, "What's so wrong about enjoying my comfort zone?" Nothing. But remember, the risk of riskless living is the greatest risk of all. Try something new today. In the graphic above, fill in the things that take courage, and the things in your comfort zone.

Habit 3: Put First Things First

Week 23

The Time Quadrants

	URGENT	NOT URGENT
IMPORTANT	**1. THE PROCRASTINATOR** • Exam Tomorrow • Friend Gets Injured • Late for Work • Project Due Today • Car Breaks Down	**2. THE PRIORITIZER** • Planning, Goal Setting • Essay Due in a Week • Exercise • Relationships • Relaxation
NOT IMPORTANT	**3. THE YES-PERSON** • Unimportant Phone Calls • Interruptions • Other People's Small Problems • Peer Pressure	**4. THE SLACKER** • Too Much TV • Endless Phone Calls • Excessive Computer Games • Mall Marathons • Time Wasters

Habit 3: Put First Things First

Ask yourself:

Where do I spend my time?

	URGENT	NOT URGENT
IMPORTANT	1. THE PROCRASTINATOR	2. THE PRIORITIZER
NOT IMPORTANT	3. THE YES-PERSON	4. THE SLACKER

Identify where you spend your time in a typical day. Be honest with yourself.

Habit 3: Put First Things First

Week 24

Packing More into Your Life

The better you organize yourself and your time, the more you'll be able to pack in—more time for family and friends, more time for school, more time for yourself, more time for your most important things—for what matters most to you.

Habit 3: Put First Things First

Ask yourself:

Where do I spend the majority of my time? Am I a procrastinator? Do I say yes to things and people even when I want to say no? Am I a slacker—do I waste a great deal of my day doing meaningless things?

Think of something you've procrastinated for a long time but that is important to you or really needs to be done. Make a plan, block out the time, and get it done this week.

Week 25

Time Quadrant Challenge

Identify your Big Rocks. At the end or beginning of each week, sit down and think about what you want to accomplish for the upcoming week.

Habit 3: Put First Things First

Ask yourself:

What are the most important things I need to do this week? (These are your Big Rocks.)

Block out time on this weekly calendar page for your Big Rocks. Then schedule in everything else. Keep your commitments to the Big Rocks for one week.

MON	TUE	WED	THU
FRI	SAT	SUN	

Habit 3: Put First Things First

Week 26

The Public Victory

The Private Victory helps you become independent so that you can say, "I am responsible for myself and my actions." The Public Victory will help you learn to work cooperatively with others, so that you can say, "I am a team player and I have influence with people."

Your ability to get along with others will largely determine how successful you are in your career and your level of personal happiness.

Private Victory to Public Victory

Ask yourself:

As I consider all my relationships—family, friends, teachers, classmates—do others look to me for direction? Or am I tossed to and fro by opinions and trends?

Consider what the following quote means to you, and how you can apply it in your life.

"What the superior man seeks is in himself; what the small man seeks is in others."

—Confucius

Private Victory to Public Victory

Week 27

Relationship Bank Account

Why is success with self (Private Victory) so important to success with others (Public Victory)? If you're struggling in your relationships, you probably don't have to look any further than yourself for the answer. The Relationship Bank Account represents the amount of trust and confidence you have in each of your relationships.

Private Victory to Public Victory

Ask yourself:

Do I break promises? Do I do small acts of kindness for others? Do I talk about friends and family behind their backs? Do I apologize when I'm in the wrong?

Before you go to bed tonight, write two notes: one a note of apology to someone you may have offended and one note of gratitude to someone who did something for you.

Private Victory to Public Victory

Practicing the Private Victory

Week 28

"Remember always that you not only have the right to be an individual, you have an obligation to be one."
—Eleanor Roosevelt

Private Victory to Public Victory

Ask yourself:

What's it like to be in a relationship with you? If you had to rate how well you're doing in your most important relationships, how would you score?

How are your relationships with...	Lousy				Excellent
Your friends?	1	2	3	4	5
Your siblings?	1	2	3	4	5
Your parents or guardian?	1	2	3	4	5
Your romantic partner?	1	2	3	4	5
Your teachers?	1	2	3	4	5

Private Victory to Public Victory

Habit 4: Think Win-Win

Habit 4: Think Win-Win is an attitude toward life, a mental frame of mind that says I can win, and so can you. It's not me or you, it's both of us. It begins with the belief that we are all equal, that no one is inferior or superior to anyone else.

Ask yourself:

Am I truly happy for my friend even if they get the position on the team I wanted? Do I feel inferior if my friends wear nicer clothes or drive newer cars than I do?

Look for Win-Win thinking in your life—you may have pitched in to help after a party; maybe you shared the credit when you scored a goal in soccer; or you spent extra time practicing with your group before a band or orchestra concert so that the whole group sounds amazing. Give yourself credit for what you are already doing well.

Week 30

The 4 Mindsets

Win-Lose: You have to come out on top or else you're weak.

Lose-Win: The other person gets what they want, but you're left without.

Lose-Lose: You can't compromise, so neither of you gets anything.

Win-Win: You find a middle ground where you each compromise, but both of you can still win.

Habit 4: Think Win-Win

Ask yourself:

How do I view life? Is everything a competition I have to win? Or do I give in just to keep the peace?

If you play sports or games, show good sportsmanship. Compliment your opponent for a game well played.

Habit 4: Think Win-Win

Week 31

Competing

Competition is healthy when you compete against yourself, or when it challenges you to reach and stretch. Competition becomes harmful when you tie your self-worth to winning or when you use it as a way to place yourself above another.

Habit 4: Think Win-Win

Ask yourself:

Do I use competition as a benchmark to measure myself rather than measuring others? Do I compete for the sake of winning or showing off?

Without caring whether you win or lose, play a game with others just for the fun of it. Don't keep score.

Habit 4: Think Win-Win

Week 32

Comparing

Comparing is competition's twin. We are all on different timetables—socially, mentally, and physically. Since we all bake differently, we shouldn't keep opening the oven door to see how well our cake is baking compared to our neighbor's, or own cake won't rise at all.

Habit 4: Think Win-Win

Ask yourself:

Do I base my self-worth on how I stack up compared to others? Do I feel more secure when my GPA is higher than someone else's? Or, do I feel like a failure because my GPA isn't even close to the highest in the class? Do I dwell on comparisons with others?

Pinpoint an area of life where you most struggle with comparisons—perhaps it's clothing, physical features, friends, or talents. Devise a plan to overcome that comparison-thinking.

Week 33

The Benefits of a Win-Win Spirit

Those who are committed to helping others succeed will become a magnet for friends. Think about it. Don't you just love people who are interested in your success and want you to win? Further, thinking abundantly opens up more possibilities for you, too.

Habit 4: Think Win-Win

Ask yourself:

When was the last time I helped someone else succeed? How did that feel?

Think of your general attitude toward life. Is it based on Win-Win thinking? How is this attitude affecting you?

Habit 4: Think Win-Win

Week 34

Habit 5: Seek First to Understand...

The key to communication and having power and influence with people can be summed up in one sentence: Seek first to understand, then to be understood. In other words, listen first, talk second. If you can learn this simple habit—to see things from another's point of view before sharing your own—a whole new world of understanding will be opened up to you.

Habit 5: Seek First to Understand, Then to Be Understood

Ask yourself:

What is my deepest need? Is it to be heard and understood? Can I apply that same need to someone else and see things from their point of view before sharing my own?

The next time you are in a heated and emotional discussion with someone, consciously look for what they are saying behind the words. Repeat it back to them until they are satisfied that you truly understand their point of view.

Week 35

Then Seek to Be Understood

Seeking first to understand requires consideration. Then to be understood requires courage. The second half of Habit 5, Then Seek to Be Understood, is as important as the first half.

Habit 5: Seek First to Understand, Then to Be Understood

Ask yourself:

Do I give feedback in a way that can be seen as a deposit into another's RBA (Relationship Bank Account)? Do I give honest feedback without an agenda and do I deliver it constructively?

Think of a situation where your constructive and kind feedback might really help another person. When the time is right, and with their permission, share the feedback with them.

Week 36

Five Poor Listening Styles

When people talk, we seldom listen because we're usually too busy preparing a response, or filtering words through our own paradigms. We tend to use one of five poor listening styles:

1) Spacing out
2) Pretend listening
3) Selective listening
4) Word listening
5) Self-centered listening

Habit 5: Seek First to Understand, Then to Be Understood

Ask yourself:

Which of the five poor listening styles do I have the biggest problem with? Do I interrupt, do I judge, do I pretend to listen?

The next time you're in a mall, park, or school cafeteria, watch how people communicate with each other. Observe what their body language is saying.

Week 37

Genuine Listening

There is a higher form of listening which is called "genuine listening." Genuine listening requires three things:

1) Listening with your eyes, heart, and ears

2) Standing in their shoes

3) Practicing mirroring

Habit 5: Seek First to Understand, Then to Be Understood

Ask yourself:

Do I look at conversations as competitions? Where it's my point of view against theirs? Do I consider that we both can be right because we each have our own point of view and paradigms?

Sometime this week, ask your mom, dad, or guardian, "How's it going?" Open up your heart and practice genuine listening.

Habit 5: Seek First to Understand, Then to Be Understood

Week **38**

Stand in Their Shoes

Think like a mirror. What does a mirror do? It doesn't judge. It doesn't give advice. It reflects. Mirroring is simply this: repeat back in your own words what the other person is saying and feeling.

Habit 5: Seek First to Understand, Then to Be Understood

Ask yourself:

In a heated discussion, is it my attitude and desire to really understand the other person?

When trying to genuinely listen, try using these phrases:

"It sounds like you feel..."
"So, what you're saying is..."

Continue the mirroring phrases until the other person feels understood.

Habit 5: Seek First to Understand, Then to Be Understood

Week 39

Listening and Reflecting

What does this quote mean to me?

"I need to listen well so that I hear what is not said."

—Thuli Madonsela

Habit 5: Seek First to Understand, Then to Be Understood

Ask yourself:

Who do I need to genuinely listen to?
How do I choose to listen differently?

This week, pay close attention to the conversations you have with one particular person. Note how they have changed since you became aware of how to listen effectively.

Habit 5: Seek First to Understand, Then to Be Understood

Habit 6: Synergize

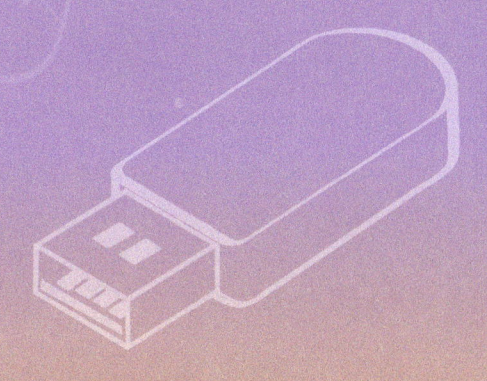

Week 40

Synergy is achieved when two or more people work together to create a better solution than either could alone. It's not your way or my way but a better way, a higher way.

Habit 6: Synergize

Ask yourself:

What roadblocks get in my way to celebrating differences? Am I part of a clique? Am I biased?

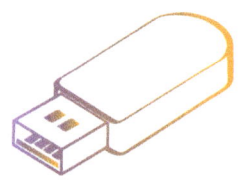

Go out of your way to get involved with people who aren't part of your "inner circle." Make new friends and get involved in a project that reaches out to new people in your school.

Week 41

Celebrating Differences

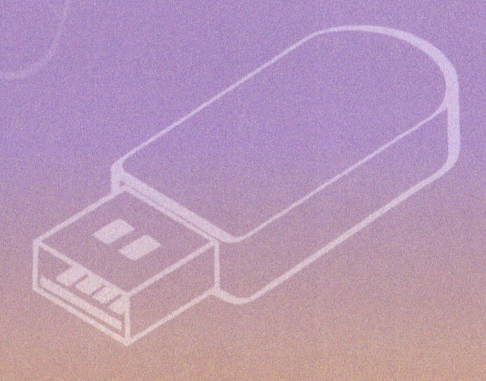

Synergy is a process. And the foundation of getting there is to celebrate differences. Celebrators value differences. They've learned that two people who think differently can achieve more than two people who think alike.

Habit 6: Synergize

Ask yourself:

Do I tend to avoid or dislike people whose opinions are different from mine? Do I tend to avoid or dislike people who look different from me?

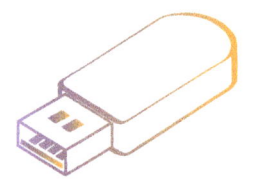

Think about someone who irritates you. What is different about them? Find out what you can learn from them and take the time to get to know them.

Week 42

Finding the "High" Way

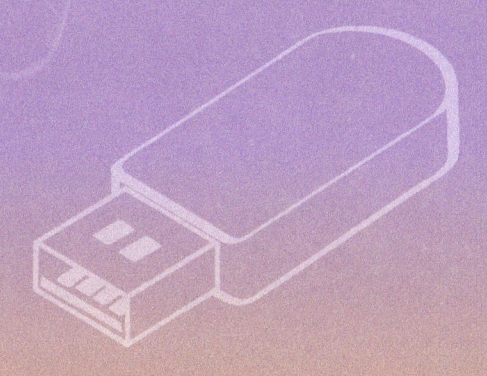

Once you've understood that differences are a strength and not a weakness, you're ready to find the High Way. Synergy is more than compromise or cooperation. Synergy is 1+1= 3 or more. It is creative cooperation and the whole is greater than the sum of the parts.

Habit 6: Synergize

Ask yourself:

Do I have the maturity to synergize with others? Do I have the patience to listen to the other point of view? Do I have the courage to express my point of view in a respectful manner?

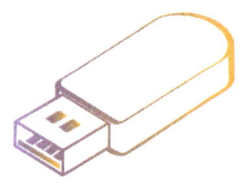

Brainstorm with friends and come up with a list of fun, new, and out of the ordinary things (safe and legal!) to do this weekend. Listen to everyone's ideas. Choose an idea, not your own, and do it.

Habit 6: Synergize

Week 43

Getting to Synergy

Synergy Action Plan

- ☐ Define the problem or opportunity
- ☐ Understand Their Way (Seek first to understand the ideas of others.)
- ☐ Explain My Way (Seek to be understood by sharing your ideas.)
- ☐ Brainstorm (Create new options and ideas.)
- ☐ Find the High Way (Find the best solution.)

Habit 6: Synergize

Ask yourself:

How did it feel to try the Synergy Action Plan? Have I noticed a difference in the relationship?

_____
_____
_____
_____
_____
_____
_____
_____
_____

Habit 6: Synergize

Week 44

Habit 7: Sharpen the Saw

Habit 7 is all about keeping your personal self sharp so that you can better deal with life. It means regularly renewing and strengthening the four key dimensions of your life—your body, your brain, your heart, and your soul.

Habit 7: Sharpen the Saw

Ask yourself:

Have I neglected a dimension of my life? Am I in balance physically, mentally, emotionally, and spiritually?

Just like a guitar, you too need regular tune-ups. You need time out to rejuvenate YOU. Right now take a self-assessment of your four dimensions.

Week 45

The 4 Dimensions of You

The four key ingredients to a healthy body are good sleeping habits, good nutrition, physical relaxation, and proper exercise. Listen to your body—be moderate and avoid extremes.

Habit 7: Sharpen the Saw

Ask yourself:

What is my body telling me right now? Did I get enough sleep last night? Have I eaten any fruits or vegetables today?

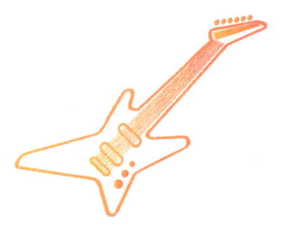

For a full week get at *least* seven hours of sleep each night.

Habit 7: Sharpen the Saw

Week 46

Caring for Your Body

This ever-changing body of yours is really quite a marvelous machine. You can handle it with care or you can abuse it. You can control it or let it control you. Your body is a gift, and if you take good care of it, it will serve you well.

Habit 7: Sharpen the Saw

Ask yourself:

What unhealthy addictions do I have? Are those addictions controlling my life?

Give up a bad habit for a week. Go without soda, alcohol, fried foods, chocolate, cigarettes, or whatever else may be hurting your body.

Habit 7: Sharpen the Saw

Week **47**

Caring for Your Brain

Perhaps more than anything else, what you do with that mass of gray material between your ears will determine your future. The mental dimension of Sharpen the Saw means developing brain power through school, extracurricular activities, hobbies, job, and other mind-enlarging experiences.

Habit 7: Sharpen the Saw

Ask yourself:

What do I need to do to achieve my future career goals? Am I working on those goals now?

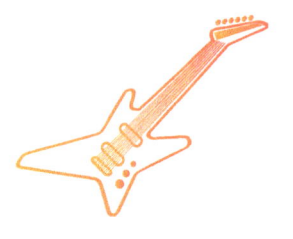

Interview someone who has a career in the field you are interested in. Do some research on what is required to get a job in this field.

Habit 7: Sharpen the Saw

Week 48

Caring for Your Heart

The best way to nourish your heart is to focus on building relationships by making regular deposits into your Relationship Bank Accounts and your own Personal Bank Account.

Habit 7: Sharpen the Saw

Ask yourself:

If I did an inventory of my closest relationships, are there any that may have too many withdrawals? Am I in the "red" on any of them? Are any of those relationships really strong and healthy?

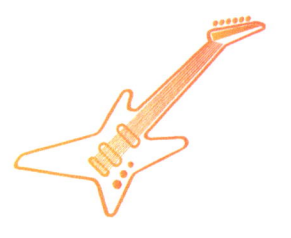

If you've made a promise to a member of your family and you have not yet kept it, go to them and apologize, then set clear expectations about when you'll do it and how you'll do it.

Week 49

Caring for Your Soul

Your soul is your center, wherein lies your deepest convictions and values. It is the source for purpose, meaning, and inner peace. Sharpening the saw in the spiritual part of life means taking time to renew and awaken that inner self.

Habit 7: Sharpen the Saw

Ask yourself:

What deeply inspires me? Music, nature, service, poetry, worship services, meditation?

Every day for thirty days, take five minutes to meditate, practice mindfulness, or do deep breathing exercises.

Habit 7: Sharpen the Saw

Week 50

My 4 Dimensions

Body – Caring for your body in a healthy way with balanced exercise, sleep, and nutrition.

Brain – Challenging your mind with new activities, learning new skills, and daring to step outside of your comfort zone.

Heart – Nourishing the relationship you have with yourself and others.

Soul – Taking time for yourself to focus inward, relax, and renew.

Habit 7: Sharpen the Saw

Ask yourself:

What are my goals for each dimension?

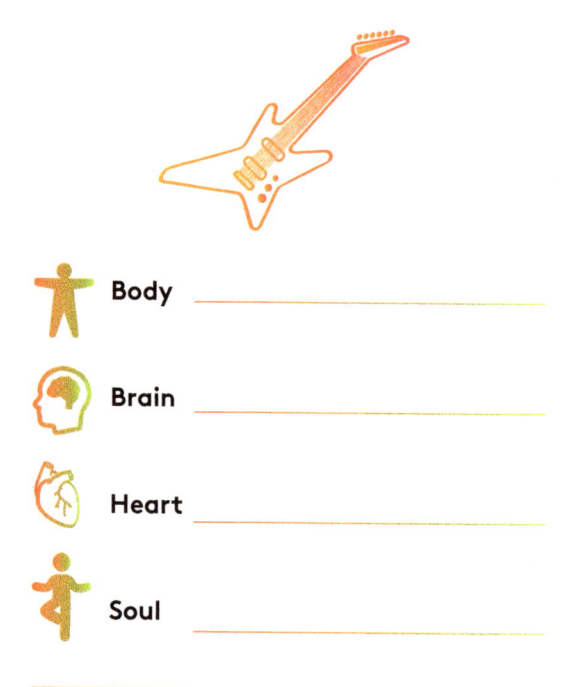

Body _____

Brain _____

Heart _____

Soul _____

Habit 7: Sharpen the Saw

Week 51

Keep Hope Alive

If you ever find yourself sliding or falling short, don't get discouraged. Remember the flight of an airplane. A plane is off course much of the time. The key is that the pilots keep making course corrections. As a result, a plane reaches its destination. Keep making your own small adjustments and keep hope alive—you'll eventually reach your destination.

Conclusion

Ask yourself:

What habit or principle had the greatest impact on me? What habit did I feel the strongest need to work on?

Whichever habit was most powerful for you, teach it to someone else in your own words. Share what you learned and the progress you have made.

Conclusion

Week 52

Now What?

You'll want to apply these habits to the most important decisions you'll have to make about school, your relationship with your parents, dating and sex, addictions, and your self-worth.

Conclusion

Ask yourself:

How can I ensure the greatest chance for success in life? Do I want to be successful in life? Why?

Read the book *The 6 Most Important Decisions You'll Ever Make* by Sean Covey to build on these new habits you've created and push yourself further to an even more effective and inspiring life.

Conclusion

Bonus Features

Finding Your Purpose

"How different our lives are when we really know what is deeply important to us, and, keeping that picture in mind, we manage ourselves each day to be and to do what really matters most."

—Stephen R. Covey

When I was a guest speaker in an elementary classroom many years ago, I asked the little kids, "So what do you want to be when you grow up?" They said:

"I want to be one of those guys in the brown trucks who bring boxes to your house." —Nathan, 6

"I want to be happy." —Mariah, 10

"I really really, really, really want to be a computer tech guy." —Michael, 11

"I want to be a photographer and travel everywhere, maybe even space." —Daysa, 10

Bonus Features

I can't believe I asked that question more than fourteen years ago, and now all those "little kids" are grown up.

I later ran into Daysa's mother who reported that Daysa was a photographer at the White House and she has traveled everywhere—but not yet to space.

This experience has taught me that the key to life is finding your purpose. I'm talking about finding your groove, your niche. What you were born to do. Daysa figured this out at the age of ten—she found her purpose and she's now living her dream. It's never too early, or too late, to tap into what you were born to do.

So how can you do the same?

Imagine four circles.

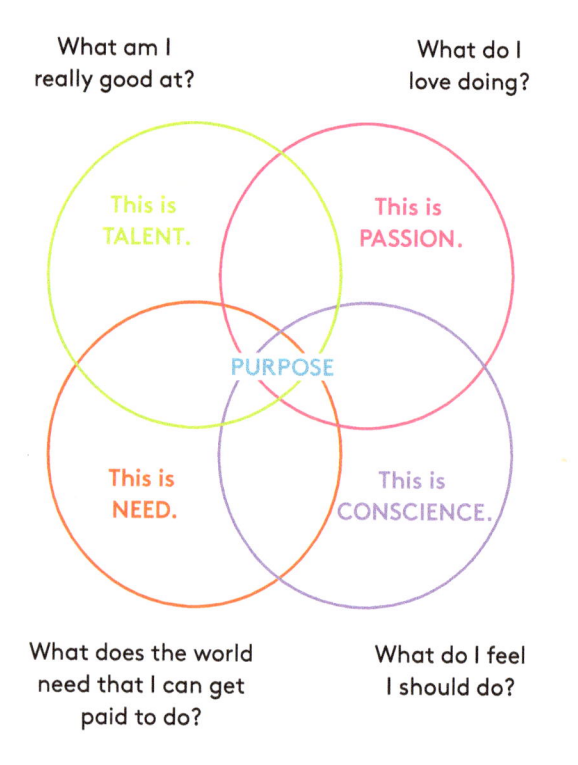

What am I really good at?

What do I love doing?

This is TALENT.

This is PASSION.

PURPOSE

This is NEED.

This is CONSCIENCE.

What does the world need that I can get paid to do?

What do I feel I should do?

And where these four circles intersect represents your purpose.

Bonus Features

To help you further discover your purpose, try the Purpose Finder activity on the next couple of pages.

Talent

1. What am I really good at?
2. What can I do better than most?
3. What would those who know me best say my greatest strengths are?
4. Of all the jobs listed here, the three that I'd be best at (or add your own):

Accountant	Engineer
Firefighter	Teacher
Computer Programmer	Therapist
	Photographer
Nurse	Pilot
Mechanic	Store Owner
Surgeon	Truck Driver
Farmer	Artist
Lawyer	Dentist
Architect	Salesperson
Policeman	Veterinarian

Bonus Features

Athlete _____

Graphic Designer _____

Homemaker _____

Child Care Provider _____

Writer _____

Passion

1. What do I enjoy most about school?
2. What subject do I enjoy most at school?
3. If money were no obstacle, what would I spend my time doing?
4. If I could be famous for something, what would it be?

Need

1. Where is there a need in the world that I could meet?
2. What is the big need in my family right now and how can I help?
3. Among my friends, who is in great need now and how can I help?
4. What skills do I have that people would be willing to pay for?

Bonus Features

Conscience

1. How can I best help and serve others?
2. What do I feel that life is asking of me?
3. Is there something I have always felt I should do with my life, even though I've ignored these thoughts in the past?
4. What single thing could be my downfall if I'm not careful?

Your Life's Work

If you're still totally confused about what you want to be when you grow up, relax. There's no rush. You don't have to decide your profession, your major, or anything today. Just be on the lookout. Become aware of what your life's mission and purpose might be. Take note of what you're good at.

When you were born, your life's work was born with you. In other words, you need to believe each of us has a purpose and a special something we need to do.

You have unique talents and gifts that no one else has. And surely there's something special you can do with your life that no one else can. There are so many ways to serve and make contribution at school, at work, and at home.

Writing a mission statement can be a great way to express your purpose. To build your own unique personal mission statement online, visit msb.franklincovey.com.

I wish you great success, and fun, on your journey.

SEAN COVEY

Bonus Features

Mission Statement Builder

"How different our lives are when we really know what is deeply important to us, and, keeping that picture in mind, we manage ourselves each day to be and to do what really matters most."

—Stephen R. Covey

As I debated on what bonus features to add to this book, I asked myself, "What will have the greatest influence on my reader and on their future?" And then I remembered when my colleague, Annie, once shared this story:

> "I taught the 7 Habits at a local community college for several years. It was an incredible experience teaching these young people, and not-so-young, non-traditional students, about the power of habits, goals, and principles.

As their teacher and friend, I was curious about the impact of the content and the habits on the students. I wanted to know where they felt the greatest connection and the greatest return on their time by taking this class. So, I added a 'freebie' question to the final exam. I wanted to give the students an opportunity to share honestly—and every test should include a freebie question, shouldn't it? No one should totally fail every question on a test unless they simply don't take it.

The question at the end of the final exam was, 'What is your favorite habit and why?' I was very surprised to discover that an overwhelming majority of the students chose Habit 2: Begin with the End in Mind. The reasons varied, but a central theme came through: this was the first time most of these students had plotted out a course for their future. Some, not all, had plotted a course for college and what they wanted to study and embrace as a profession, but many were in college only because it was expected. About 99 percent of my college students had no life vision—no driving purpose, no life contribution, no life mission.

I was totally stunned when semester after semester, my students voiced the same thing at the end of the course—'I NOW finally have a purpose and meaning to my life.'

I think I was so surprised because I had chosen my life goals at a young age—I don't know why or what drove me to focus on goals, but somehow I did and just assumed that everyone else did, too."

This experience is likely not uncommon. There are many who have not specifically defined what contribution they want to make in life, or what their driving purpose will be. For this reason, I felt it important to provide a means of doing this. Even if you have defined your life goals at an earlier time, like Annie, this could be an exercise that reinspires you to stay on track. Who knows? Your goals might even change.

Please enjoy the following thoughts and ideas and, as you read, ask yourself these questions:

- Have I defined my purpose in life?
- Am I aware of what I uniquely can do that others can't or won't do?
- What and who do I want to be in my life?
- What principles and values do I want to live my life by?
- What will be my legacy?

Use everything you learned in this book to help you build your mission statement and become the most effective person you can be. Your effectiveness can change the world.

The Editor

"Writing or reviewing a mission statement changes you because it forces you to think through your priorities deeply, carefully, and to align your behavior with your beliefs. As you do, other people begin to sense that you're not being driven by everything that happens to you."

—Stephen R. Covey

Bonus Features

The Crossroads of Life

Let's take a look at the first important reason to have an end in mind. So here you are. You're young. You're free. You have your whole life before you. You're standing at the crossroads of life and you have to choose which paths to take.

> Do you want to go to college or graduate school?
>
> What will your attitude toward life be?
>
> Should you try out for that team?
>
> What type of friends do you want to have?
>
> Will you join a gang?
>
> Who will you date?
>
> Will you have sex before marriage?
>
> Will you drink, smoke, do drugs?
>
> What values will you choose?

Bonus Features

> What kind of relationships do you want with your family?
>
> What will you stand for?
>
> How will you contribute to your community?

The paths you choose today can shape you forever. It's both frightening and exciting that we have to make so many vital decisions when we're so young, but such is life. Imagine an eighty-foot rope stretched out before you. Each foot represents one year of your life. Teenagehood is only seven years, such a short span of rope, but those seven affect the remaining sixty-one, for good or bad, in such a powerful way.

Bonus Features

Mission Statement Questionnaire

Answer the following questions on the blank pages at the end of this questionnaire.

Step 1: Performance

1. I am at my best when…
2. I am at my worst when…

Step 2: Passion

1. What do I really love to do at work?
2. What do I really love to do in my personal life?

Step 3: Talents

My natural talents and gifts are:
(Examples may be art, music, decision-making, being a friend, etc.)

Bonus Features

Step 4: Imagination

If I had unlimited time and resources, and knew I could not fail, what would I choose to do?

I would:

Step 5: Vision

Imagine your life as an epic journey with you as the hero/heroine of the story. What do you imagine your journey to be about? Complete the following statement by describing what you are doing, who is it for, why you are doing it, and what the journey's results are.

1. My life's journey is…

Step 6: Character

1. Imagine your 80th birthday. Who will be there with you? What tribute statement would you like them to make about your life?

Bonus Features

Step 7: Contribution

1. What do I consider to be my most important future contribution to the most important people in my life?

Step 8: Conscience

1. Are there things I feel I really should do or change, even though I may have dismissed such thoughts many times? What are they?

Step 9: Influence

Imagine you could invite to dinner three people who have influenced you the most—past or present. Write their names in the boxes below. Then record the one quality or attribute you admire most in these people.

1. Name:
   Attribute:

2. Name:
   Attribute:

3. Name:
   Attribute:

Bonus Features

Step 10: Balance

Let's think of balance as a state of fulfillment and renewal in each of the four dimensions: physical, spiritual, mental, and social/emotional. What is the single most important thing you can do in each of these areas that will have the greatest positive impact on your life and help you achieve a sense of balance?

1. Physical:
2. Spiritual:
3. Mental:
4. Social/Emotional:

Bonus Features

Over the years, your circumstances will change. Your priorities will change. Your goals and dreams will change. That's okay—because change means growth. As you grow, transform, and broaden your horizons, allow yourself the freedom to expand and refine your mission statement.

For now, congratulate yourself on a job well done. Tell your friends about your newly stated purpose in life.

The next step is learning how to live your mission. Maybe it's easy, but maybe it takes some guidance. We're here to help. Learn more about our classes and training here: www.franklincovey. com/tc/publicworkshops.

Life is a journey. And your mission statement is your map.

Bonus Features

Bonus Features

Bonus Features

Bonus Features

Bonus Features

Bonus Features

Inspiring Thoughts on Missions and Goals

"Your mission statement becomes your constitution, the solid expression of your vision and values. It becomes the criterion by which you measure everything else in your life."

—Stephen R. Covey

"To the person who does not know where he wants to go there is no favorable wind."

—Seneca

"My mission in life is not merely to survive, but to thrive; and to do so with some passion, some compassion, some humor, and some style."

—Maya Angelou

Bonus Features

"If you're proactive you don't have to wait for circumstances or other people to create perspective-expanding experiences. You can consciously create your own."

—Stephen R. Covey

"Whatever life holds in store for me, I will never forget these words, 'With great power comes great responsibility.' This is my gift, my curse. Who am I? I am Spider-Man"

—Peter Parker, *Spider-Man*

"Stay focused on the mission."

—Naveen Jain

"Here is a test to find whether your mission on Earth is finished: If you're alive, it isn't."

—Richard Bach

Bonus Features

"A mission statement is not something you write overnight. It takes deep introspection, careful analysis, thoughtful expression, and often many rewrites to produce it in final form. It may take you several weeks or even months before you feel really comfortable with it, before you feel it is a complete and concise expression of your innermost values and directions."

—Stephen R. Covey

"Would you tell me, please, which way I ought to go from here?" "That depends a good deal on where you want to get to," said the Cat. "I don't much care where—" said Alice. "Then it doesn't matter which way you go," said the Cat.

—Lewis Carroll, *Alice in Wonderland*

Bonus Features

"I've always been inspired by women, and my mission was to inspire women. I always wanted to become a certain kind of woman, and I became that woman through fashion. It was a dialogue. I would see that the wrap dress made those women confident, and made them act with confidence."

—Diane von Furstenberg

"How different our lives are when we really know what is deeply important to us, and keeping that picture in mind, we manage ourselves each day to be and to do what really matters most."

—Stephen R. Covey

"A personal mission statement is like a tree with deep roots. It is stable and isn't going anywhere but it is also alive and continually growing."

—Sean Covey

Bonus Features

"The bigger your mission becomes, the greater inspiration you will be given."

—Ryuho Okawa

"By having a clear vision, even a short vision of what will happen in the future. We will be less worried and feel a little bit confident, and calm because we can manage our life in the world that is changing every second."

—Ly Nguyen

Bonus Features

Affirmations on the Go

Here are some affirmations to keep you focused on your mission, and remind you of the power of the habits. As you work on each habit, take one of these affirmations and repeat it to yourself throughout the day. Make it your focus, and watch your perspective change.

Habit 1: Be Proactive

My ability to conquer my challenges is limitless; my potential to succeed is infinite.

I wake up every morning feeling positive and enthusiastic about life.

I carry my own weather.

I am mindful of my language. I avoid reactive language.

I face my failures head-on. The only failure is giving up. I learn from my failures.

I recognize resistance as merely an obstacle, not a roadblock.

I face my fears head on. I learn from them.

I push pause and think before reacting to an emotional or difficult situation.

Habit 2: Begin with the End in Mind

I am willing to explore new and uncharted territory.

I am the architect of my life; I build its foundation and choose its contents.

I live by my mission. I follow the beat of my inner drummer. I will be myself, not what others want me to be.

I invest my time, talents, abilities, and life in those activities which fulfill my ultimate purpose.

I am the captain of my ship; I chart my own course and choose my own cargo.

I refer back to my mission statement whenever I am faced with important life decisions.

I frequently ask myself: "Is the life I'm living leading me in the right direction?"

Habit 3: Put First Things First

My mind is energized, clear, and focused on the process of my goals.

My daily goals will ensure I reach my long term goals.

For today, I am truly attentive to my work. I will be observant and attentive throughout the day.

Today I will spend time strengthening relationships.

I turn my dreams into goals. I turn my goals into steps. I turn my steps into actions. I complete an action every day.

I will prepare today for future crises.

I concentrate all my efforts on the things I want to accomplish in life.

I spend my time focused on what matters most.

Bonus Features

Habit 4: Think Win-Win

I face difficult situations with a balance of courage and consideration. I will find solutions in these difficult times.

In seeking for Win-Win I focus on the issues, not the personalities or positions.

I am genuinely happy for the success of others.

My abundance mentality flows out of my own deep inner sense of personal worth and security.

I choose a Win-Win frame of mind and heart that constantly seeks mutual benefit in all human interaction.

I confidently practice Win-Win as a habit of interpersonal leadership.

When others are scripted in Win-Lose, I balance courage with consideration in finding mutual benefit.

Habit 5: Seek First to Understand, Then to Be Understood

I listen reflectively without judgment to gain complete understanding.

I choose to see things from another's point of view before sharing my own.

The deepest need of the human heart is to be understood.

I listen with my heart, my eyes, and then my ears.

I show my level of care and commitment by empathically listening.

I am mindful of timing and my choice of words when I give feedback.

I practice patience and understanding with others and myself.

Habit 6: Synergize

I am a problem solver. I work with others to find the very best solutions.

I celebrate diversity and I value differences in people and ideas.

In my personal relationships, I strive for the ideal environment for synergy—a high emotional

bank account, think Win-Win, and seek first to understand. I am committed to working with others to create a better solution.

I keep my mind open to the possibilities of teamwork and communication.

There is an abundance of benefit, recognition, and success to go around for everyone.

Habit 7: Sharpen the Saw

I am fit, healthy, and full of self-confidence. My outer self is matched by my inner well-being.

I have strength in my heart and clarity in my mind.

I seek balance in the four dimensions of my life: physical, mental, spiritual, and social/emotional.

I am calm and relaxed which energizes my whole being.

Life is an upward spiral of learn, commit, do, and learn, commit, and do over and over again.

My body is a marvelous machine. I handle it with care and I don't abuse it.

I look for ways to build others up rather than to tear them down.

I find peace and calm in nature.

I use my gift of imagination to clearly visualize the attainment of my goals.

Bonus Features

Sean Covey

Sean Covey is a business executive, author, speaker, and innovator. He is President of FranklinCovey Education and is devoted to transforming education throughout the world. Sean oversees FranklinCovey's whole school transformation process, called Leader in Me, which is now in over 4,000 schools and 50 countries throughout the world.

Sean is a *New York Times* best-selling author and has authored or co-authored several books, including the *Wall Street Journal* #1 Business Bestseller, *The 4 Disciplines of Execution*, *The 6 Most Important Decisions You'll Ever Make*, *The 7 Habits of Happy Kids*, *The Leader in Me*, and *The 7 Habits of Highly Effective Teens*, which has been translated into 30 languages and sold over 5 million copies worldwide. He is a versatile keynoter who regularly speaks to youth and adults.

Sean graduated with honors from BYU with a Bachelor's degree in English and later earned his MBA from Harvard Business School. As the starting quarterback for BYU, he led his team to two bowl games and was twice selected as the ESPN Most Valuable Player of the Game.

Sean and his family founded and run a global, non-profit charity called Bridle Up Hope whose mission is to inspire hope, confidence, and resilience in at-risk young women through equestrian training.

Sean and his wife, Rebecca, live with their children in Alpine, Utah.

Copyright © 2021 FranklinCovey Co.

Published by Mango Publishing Group
Mango is an active supporter of authors' rights to free speech and artistic expression in their books. The purpose of copyright is to encourage authors to produce exceptional works that enrich our culture and our open society.

Uploading or distributing photos, scans or any content from this book without prior permission is theft of the author's intellectual property. Please honor the author's work as you would your own. Thank you in advance for respecting our author's rights.

For permission requests, please contact the publisher at:
FranklinCovey Co.
2200 W. Parkway Blvd.
Salt Lake City, UT 84119
Attn: Annie Oswald

For special orders, quantity sales, course adoptions and corporate sales, please email the publisher at sales@mango.bz. For trade and wholesale sales, please contact Ingram Publisher Services at customer.service@ingramcontent.com or +1.800.509.4887.

The 7 Habits of Highly Effective Teens on the Go

ISBN: (print) 978-1-64250-652-5, (ebook) 978-1-64250-653-2
BISAC: YAN029000—YOUNG ADULT NONFICTION / Inspirational & Personal Growth

Printed in the United States

FRANKLINCOVEY
ON LEADERSHIP

WITH
SCOTT MILLER

Join executive vice president Scott Miller for weekly interviews with thought leaders, bestselling authors, and world-renowned experts on the topics of organizational culture, leadership development, execution, and personal productivity.

FEATURED INTERVIEWS INCLUDE:

GUY KAWASAKI
WISE GUY

SUSAN DAVID
EMOTIONAL AGILITY

KIM SCOTT
RADICAL CANDOR

DANIEL PINK
WHEN

SETH GODIN
THE DIP, LINCHPIN, PURPLE COW

JEAN CHATZKY
AGEPROOF

LIZ WISEMAN
MULTIPLIERS

RACHEL HOLLIS
GIRL, WASH YOUR FACE

STEPHEN M. R. COVEY
THE SPEED OF TRUST

NANCY DUARTE
DATA STORY, SLIDE:OLOGY

SUSAN CAIN
THE QUIET REVOLUTION

STEPHANIE McMAHON
CHIEF BRAND OFFICER, WWE

GENERAL STANLEY McCHRYSTAL
LEADERS: MYTH AND REALITY

CHRIS McCHESNEY
THE 4 DISCIPLINES OF EXECUTION

Subscribe to FranklinCovey's *On Leadership* to receive weekly videos, tools, articles, and podcasts at

FRANKLINCOVEY.COM/ONLEADERSHIP.

© Franklin Covey Co. All rights reserved.

FranklinCovey
ALL ACCESS PASS

The FranklinCovey All Access Pass provides unlimited access to our best-in-class content and solutions, allowing you to expand your reach, achieve your business objectives, and sustainably impact performance across your organization.

AS A PASSHOLDER, YOU CAN:

- Access FranklinCovey's world-class content, whenever and wherever you need it, including *The 7 Habits of Highly Effective People®: Signature Edition 4.0*, *Leading at the Speed of Trust®*, and *The 5 Choices to Extraordinary Productivity®*.

- Certify your internal facilitators to teach our content, deploy FranklinCovey consultants, or use digital content to reach your learners with the behavior-changing content you require.

- Have access to a certified implementation specialist who will help design impact journeys for behavior change.

- Organize FranklinCovey content around your specific business-related needs.

- Build a common learning experience throughout your entire global organization with our core-content areas, localized into 16 languages.

- Join thousands of organizations using the All Access Pass to implement strategy, close operational gaps, increase sales, drive customer loyalty, and improve employee engagement.

To learn more, visit

FRANKLINCOVEY.COM or call **1-888-868-1776.**

FranklinCovey.
THE ULTIMATE COMPETITIVE ADVANTAGE

© Franklin Covey Co. All rights reserved.

Mango Publishing, established in 2014, publishes an eclectic list of books by diverse authors—both new and established voices—on topics ranging from business, personal growth, women's empowerment, LGBTQ studies, health, and spirituality to history, popular culture, time management, decluttering, lifestyle, mental wellness, aging, and sustainable living. We were recently named 2019 *and* 2020's #1 fastest growing independent publisher by *Publishers Weekly*. Our success is driven by our main goal, which is to publish high quality books that will entertain readers as well as make a positive difference in their lives.

Our readers are our most important resource; we value your input, suggestions, and ideas. We'd love to hear from you—after all, we are publishing books for you!

Please stay in touch with us and follow us at:
Facebook: Mango Publishing
Twitter: @MangoPublishing
Instagram: @MangoPublishing
LinkedIn: Mango Publishing
Pinterest: Mango Publishing

Sign up for our newsletter at www.mangopublishinggroup.com and receive a free book!

Join us on Mango's journey to reinvent publishing, one book at a time.

CPSIA information can be obtained
at www.ICGtesting.com
Printed in the USA
JSHW040037221121
20512JS00002BA/2